MEERKATS
LIFE IN THE MOB
Willow Clark

PowerKiDS press

New York

Published in 2011 by The Rosen Publishing Group, Inc.
29 East 21st Street, New York, NY 10010

Copyright © 2011 by The Rosen Publishing Group, Inc.

All rights reserved. No part of this book may be reproduced in any form without permission in writing from the publisher, except by a reviewer.

First Edition

Editor: Jennifer Way
Book Design: Julio Gil

Photo Credits: Cover, pp. 11, 17 (main, inset top, inset bottom), 23 Shutterstock.com; back cover © www.iStockphoto.com/Lee Daniels; pp. 5, 14–15, 24 (top center) Hemera/Thinkstock; pp. 7, 24 (bottom right) Stockbyte/Thinkstock; pp. 8–9 (main, inset bottom),13, 19, 20–21, 24 (top right, bottom left) iStockphoto/Thinkstock; p. 9 (inset top) Chad Baker/Photodisc/Thinkstock; p. 24 (top left) © www.iStockphoto.com/Urban Waldenström.

Library of Congress Cataloging-in-Publication Data

Clark, Willow.
 Meerkats : life in the mob / by Willow Clark. — 1st ed.
   p. cm. — (Animal families)
 Includes index.
 ISBN 978-1-4488-2511-0 (library binding) — ISBN 978-1-4488-2608-7 (pbk.) —
 ISBN 978-1-4488-2609-4 (6-pack)
 1. Meerkat—Juvenile literature. 2. Familial behavior in animals—Juvenile literature. I. Title.
 QL737.C235C573 2011
 599.74′2—dc22
                        2010019300

Manufactured in the United States of America

CPSIA Compliance Information: Batch #WW11PK: For Further Information contact Rosen Publishing, New York, New York at 1-800-237-9932

CONTENTS

A Mob of Meerkats 4
In the Burrow 10
Watching Out for Danger 18
Words to Know 24
Index 24
Web Sites 24

Meerkats live together in a group, called a **mob**.

A mob can have around 40 meerkats.

Meerkats live in the **deserts** and **grasslands** of southern Africa.

Meerkats live in **burrows** that they dig in the ground.

Living underground helps meerkats hide from animals that want to eat them.

The members of a mob take turns getting food and taking care of the babies.

Meerkats find food in the morning. They eat bugs, eggs, plants, and small animals.

One group of meerkats hunts. Another group looks out for danger.

When a guard sees danger, it makes noises. They tell the rest of the mob to hide!

Meerkats sleep in their burrow. Before sleep, they play and **groom** each other.

23

Words to Know

burrow

desert

grassland

groom

mob

Index

B
burrow(s), 10, 22

D
danger, 18, 20
deserts, 8

F
food, 14, 16

G
grasslands, 8

N
noises, 20

Web Sites

Due to the changing nature of Internet links, PowerKids Press has developed an online list of Web sites related to the subject of this book. This site is updated regularly. Please use this link to access the list:
www.powerkidslinks.com/afam/meerkat/